When I Were A Project Manager

by

Nigel Creaser

ISBN: 9781976839382

Second Edition
First Published 2015

Dedication

To my beautiful wife and two beautiful daughters, the most rewarding project of my life.

Contents

5

The players

Josiah Ramsbottom, APM

Obadiah Hardaker, PMP

Delilah Bickerstaffe, Prince II Practitioner

Ezekiel Sedgwick, MSP

The Scene

NARRATOR [WITH A DEEP RESONANT VOICE LIKE THE FELLA FROM THE BARRATT HOMES ADVERTS IN THE 1970s.]

The scene four experienced project managers sat at a hotel bar in an exclusive Project Manager retirement hotel in London's West End after delivering their final project before retirement.

"Always look on the bright side of project life" quietly playing in the background by a the string quartet in the corner.

Our hero, the wannabe Project Manager George Onaswell, serves drinks in his job as waiter, which he took to fund his long expensive journey to project management certification.

He discreetly hangs back, but ready with gin and tonic, scotch and soda, chilled Pinot Grigio, and the ever present Blue WKD. He listens with interest to the conversation, trying to pick up some tips for his future career.

We move in, to listen too.

JOSIAH:

Ahh, we did it, very pleasing.

OBADIAH:

Nothing like a project that runs smooth as clockwork, ay
Josiah?

DELILAH:

You're right there Obadiah.

EZEKIEL:

Who'd a thought thirty years ago we'd all be sittin' here
celebrating a project that ran like clockwork?

JOSIAH:

Aye. In them days, we'd a' been glad to have the price of a
first project phase.

OBADIAH:

The first WEEK of't first phase.

EZEKIEL:

Without approval or a team.

DELILAH:

OR money!

JOSIAH:

With a flakey, unclear scope.

EZEKIEL:

We never used to have a scope. We used to have to push the customer to make it up.

OBADIAH:

The best WE could manage was to make it up ourselves on a damp napkin in local pub.

DELILAH:

But you know, we were happy in those days, though we had no funding or scope.

JOSIAH:

Aye. BECAUSE we had no funding or scope. My old Mentor used to say to me, "Funding and scope does not make a project manager happy"

EZEKIEL:

'E was right. I was happier then and I had NOTHIN'. We used to have the team in a tiny office, small desks, one meeting room, with greaaaaaat big holes in our funding, and just one coffee machine.

OBADIAH:

Meeting room? You were lucky to have a meeting room! We used to work out of a corridor, all hundred and twenty-six of us, no furniture. Half the funding was missing; we were all huddled together each day for fear of one of us being LAID OFF!

DELILAH:

You were lucky to have a Corridor and Funding! *We* used to have to work from home and had no funding to do anything!

JOSIAH:

Ohhhh we used to DREAM of working from home and having no funding! Woulda' been utopia to us. Because of security we used to work in a locked shed on air base day and night.

We got woken up every morning by having a load of pointless report questions and change requests dumped on us! And we had £100k negative funding and had to pay to come to work.

EZEKIEL:

Well when I say "Office" it was only a bunch of old portaloos bolted together with the sides knocked out and the privies left in, but it was an office to US.

OBADIAH:

We were relocated from *our* privy; we had to go and work in a Starbucks using their WiFi!

DELILAH:

You were lucky to have a WiFi! There were a hundred and sixty of using a single 1,200kb dial up line and one Epson FX 1050 printer in Pronta Print down the road.

JOSIAH:

Dial up?

DELILAH:

Aye. Dial up.

JOSIAH:

You were lucky. We worked for three months in a Wimpy
near a sewage works. We used to have to get up at six
o'clock in the morning, clean the Wimpy, eat a cold two
day old burger, go to work on the project risk register
for fourteen hours a day week in-week out.

When we finished the project, the Sponsor would slate us
in our year end review and, and customer sued us for
every penny we had!

OBADIAH:

Luxury. We used to have to get to Starbucks at three
o'clock in the morning, clean it, drink a scalding hot
Double, Decaf, Skinny, Mega Milky, Chocomocha with
Sprinkles and Marshmallows, start our progress reports
and plans from scratch 10 times a day on stone tablets
using barbed wire to show dependencies and OUR Sponsor
would beat us around the head and neck with the tablets,
if we were LUCKY!

DELILAH:

Well we had it tough. We used to have to get to the office, twelve o'clock at night fire up the dial up, and type in our progress reports with our TONGUE and using our own blood to mark the red RAG status of the project.

We had half a cup of cold espresso, worked twenty-four hours a day with no holidays or training, and when we finished the project, our Sponsor would slice us in two because of the failure to meet the benefits case we had never seen.

EZEKIEL:

RIGHT! I had to send in the projects weekly progress report at 10 o'clock at night, half an hour before the previous week report had been sent, (pause for laughter), quadruple the scope every day and deliver with 1 million pounds of negative funding, work twenty-nine hours a day, without lunch or tea breaks, 9 days a week and on blue moons, pay customer for permission to deliver the project for them.[long breath]

AND when WE completed the project, our Sponsor would make us pay him to make sure he hit the benefits case, kill us and sell our organs to top up the benefits case to pay for his weekend away in Mauritius to celebrate and dance about on our graves singing "Hallelujah. Anyone can do this project management lark".

JOSIAH:

But you try and tell the young fresh faced Project
Managers today that... and they won't believe ya'.

ALL:

Nope, nope, They won't.

A concerned expression is fixed across Georges face, he
continues to serve drinks through the night enabling
horrendous hangovers the following day.

Postscript

This is obviously heavily influenced by the Four Yorkshiremen Sketch made famous by Monty Python. A bit of history of the sketch below from Wikipedia.

The origins

The "Four Yorkshiremen" sketch is a parody of nostalgic conversations about humble beginnings or difficult childhoods. Four Yorkshiremen reminisce about their upbringing, and as the conversation progresses, they try to outdo one another, their accounts of deprived childhoods becoming increasingly absurd.

The sketch was originally written and performed for the 1967 British television comedy series *At Last the 1948 Show* by the show's four writer-performers: Tim Brooke-Taylor, John Cleese, Graham Chapman and Marty Feldman.

Barry Cryer is the wine waiter in the original performance and may have contributed to the writing.

Later performances - Monty Python members

The "Four Yorkshiremen" sketch has been performed by Monty Python during their live shows, *Live at Drury Lane* (1974, no video recording available), *Live at the Hollywood Bowl* (1982) and Monty Python Live (Mostly) (2014, performed at The O_2), each performance varying slightly in its content. The performers in each case were Graham Chapman (replaced by John Cleese in the 2014 performance), Eric Idle, Terry Jones and Michael Palin (Palin is the only member of the group actually from Yorkshire). It was also performed by Cleese, Jones, Palin and Rowan Atkinson for *The Secret Policeman's Ball*, the 1979 Amnesty International benefit gala.

Performance Note

\-

If, in the unlikely event, you wish to perform this sketch at an event for your company please feel free. In return I ask a couple of things, please give me some credit, and point your attendees at thesundaylunchproject.blogspot.com.

Any unauthorised broadcasting, public performance, copying or re-recording for financial gain will constitute an infringement of copyright.

Finally if you feel I deserve a contribution for a performance of this questionable work of art please contact me at

sundaylunchpm@gmail.com

Project Management: The Sketches

A collection of classic sketches and songs with a project management twist including, Always Look on the Bright Side of Project Life, What Have Project Managers Ever Done For Us and many, many more.

Coming in 2019 ish

The Sunday Lunch Project: Are you just cooking a chicken

George Onaswell is a typical Project Manager, been delivering projects for years, adept stakeholder manager and gantt chart guru, then he gets the most terrifying high profile project of his career!

Cooking Sunday lunch for his prospective mother-in-law, head of the local Women's Institute and national roast dinner of the year champion 4 years on the trot.

How can he make it a roaring success while still delivering the thorny project he just got landed in the office? The project charter is drafted for ....

The Sunday Lunch Project!!!

What could possibly go wrong?

About the Author

———————————————

Nigel Creaser, PMI, PMQ, PSM is an experienced project and programme manager with over 20 years of varied project management roles delivering multi-million pound projects across a wide range of industries including national and regional government, financial services and telecoms and a former Director of Marketing for the Project Management Institute's UK Chapter.

He lives in North Shropshire with his wife and two daughters. When he is not managing projects or being a husband and dad you can find him on a judo mat trying to stay standing or running around trying to get a bit faster and running a little bit further.

Not blank.

Not really blank.

Still not really blank.

This one is not intentionally not left not blank.

29

Blank